FAMILY WALKS
HARTLEY WINTNI

CON

CW00429827

age

Published by
ELVETHAM PUBLICATIONS
4 Eversley Drive, Fleet, Hampshire, GU51 1BG
www.elvethampublications.co.uk
elvethampubs@aol.com

1

FAMILY WALKS SERIES

Family Walks around Hook, Hartley Wintney & Rotherwick
ISBN 978-0-9553268-0-6

Family Walks around Odiham & Beyond	2003
Family Walks around Fleet, Crookham & Crondall	2002
Family Walks around Farnham & the Hampshire Borders	2001
Family Walks around the Blackwater Valley	2000

© Elvetham Publications. All rights reserved. No part of this publication may be reproduced in any form or by any means (except short passages for review) without the prior written permission of the publisher.

Great care has been taken to be accurate. The publisher cannot however accept any responsibility for errors which may occur, or their consequences.

The walk descriptions have been checked independently, but changes can occur. **If obstructions or crops on the line of the path are encountered, please contact the Rights of Way Officer asking for the problem to be cleared. Give a map reference if possible.** Contact details are:

Rights of Way Office,
Basing House,
Redbridge lane
Basingstoke
RG24 0HB
Telephone: 0845 6035636
e-mail: rights.of.way@hants.gov.uk
web site: www.hants.gov.uk/row.htm

ABBREVIATIONS

R	Right	SP	Signpost
RHS	Right hand side	S	Stile, kissing gate or squeeze posts
L	Left	FB	Footbridge
LHS	Left hand side	W	Waymark

Fleet Bargain Bookshop

Fantastic Books at Amazing Prices Superb Selection of Books for all Ages
Adult Fiction Only £2.99 or 2 for £5 Books Ordered - Discounts Apply

245 Fleet Road,Fleet. GU51 3BP
01252 651025

INTRODUCTION

This new edition covers twelve circular walks around Hook, Hartley Wintney and Rotherwick. It includes all the walks from the previous Family Walks book, which have been revised and updated. The usual format of the walk description and its accompanying map on facing pages is retained. The paragraph numbers correspond to the numbers shown on the maps. Points of Interest seen from the walks are described separately at the end of the book.

Starting points for the walks (where parking should be available) are shown on the map in the centre pages. All of the walks can be started from any point on the walk. Ordnance Survey Explorer Map 144 at a scale of 2 $\frac{1}{2}$ miles to the inch shows all the paths in detail and walkers are encouraged to use this map although those in this book are adequate.

There are railway services to Hook and Winchfield stations. Information on public transport may be found at www.hants.gov.uk/passengertransport. Telephone: 0845 6035633

The walks pass close to public houses where refreshments are available for thirsty walkers. Please ask the landlord for his permission if you wish to leave your car in the car park (and remember to use their hospitality).

In dry conditions good walking shoes should suffice, but wellies may be needed in wetter conditions.

Some walks pass close to private houses - please respect the residences` privacy.

We would like to thank those local businesses who have helped to support this series of books by taking out advertising space. We would encourage you to use their services.

We are grateful to Bob Rose for inviting us to update the Family Walks series of books, his encouragement, guidance and support. Our thanks go to Ted Blackman for the sketch maps (based on out of copyright maps and path surveys) and to Judy Dawkins and Alison Calloway for checking the descriptions for us.

Stephen and Pam Turner
March 2008

Cover photograph front: St. Mary's Church, Hartley Wintney (by Stephen Turner) – see walk number 2 and number 3 and Points of Interest.
Cover photograph back: The Authors (by John Turner).

Walk No 1   ELVETHAM & HAZELEY HEATH

[3 $\frac{1}{4}$ miles, 1 $\frac{3}{4}$ hours]

1. Cross the road from the Lamb Hotel, Hartley Wintney and go along Park Corner Road by the golf course. At a footpath signpost on your L opposite the pond, go through squeeze posts and along the RH edge of the golf course. At the end of the gravel path, keep along the RH edge of the golf course. At the notice TO ELVETHAM pass through the bush screen and turn R along an enclosed track. Pass a small pond on the R and keep to the RH edge of the golf course.

2. Pass Footpath notice on a large oak tree on your R, go over a stile and along RH field edge to cross the next stile. Keep to the wire fence on your R to reach the footbridge. Cross the River Hart, turn L along river and then R to cross a stile at the corner of the wood. Turn L along the LH edge of the field, at the end of the wood keep ahead and go over the stile by a metal gate. Go ahead over the field heading between two large oaks to a stile by a metal gate.

3. Turn L along the road to reach and cross with great care the dualled A30. Continue along Hulfords Lane opposite. After 600 yards at a 2-fingered footpath signpost on your L, go through a kissing gate, then through a farm gate through the paddock. Go through a metal gate in the fence on the L and turn R to another metal gate, over a footbridge and through a kissing gate. Keep along LH field edge, then through a kissing gate and continue across a field to cross the River Hart on a large footbridge.

4. Bear L through the trees and cross a sleeper bridge and the bear R to a defined path across Hazeley Heath. Continue on the boardwalk and path, cross a plank footbridge, turn L and then R to join the tarmac drive passing Hatts Cottage. At Purdies Farm, turn L up the gravel track.

5. After 200 yards, turn L at concrete bollards and waymarked post on a defined path across Hazeley Heath. Ignore crossing tracks and after a few hundred yards, cross a concrete track and continue ahead on the wide gravel track. In about 250 yards at an oak tree, ignore the LH fork and keep ahead on the track ignoring side paths. Soon follow an earth path that descends through the trees. Go through a wooden gate and follow the path in front of houses. Take the enclosed path to the road; turn R and return to the Lamb Hotel.

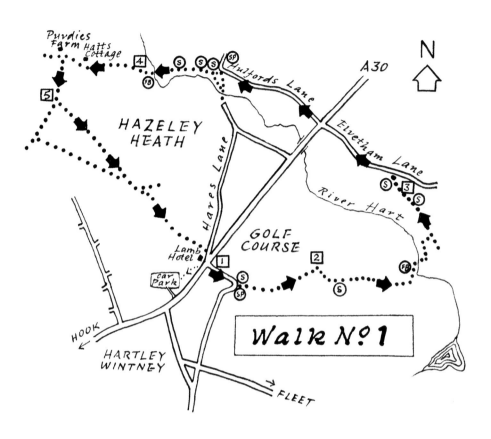

Coffees, Teas and Light Meals
Sandwiches to take-away

—o—

High Street, Hartley Wintney

Tel: (01252) 842736

Walk No 2   WEST GREEN COMMON & ST MARY'S CHURCH

[$4\frac{1}{2}$ miles, $2\frac{1}{2}$ hours]

1. Start from the Waggon & Horses, Hartley Wintney. Take the road with Hatten's Pond on your R and follow the tarmac path through the Trafalgar Oaks to reach and cross the road to the Parish Church. Turn L along the road and in a few yards take the path through the oak trees with Church Lane on your L. Keep on this road. Just beyond Meadow Way (at the footpath signpost on your L), cross the road and go through the kissing gate and along the RH field edge. Continue through squeeze posts at Wellfield House and through a kissing gate to enter St Mary's Churchyard.

2. Leave the churchyard by the gate on your R, turn L along the lay-by and go through the squeeze posts by the lychgate to pass St Mary's Church. Leave the churchyard by squeeze posts and go along the path through the trees. Cross the road to Church House Farm and turn L on the road to Winchfield. At Taplins Cottage, turn R at the footpath signpost, go along the drive and over a stile to enter a copse. At the end of the copse, cross the stile and keep ahead on the RH field edge and leave the large field by a further stile. Keep ahead (by a waymark post) through the trees and shortly turn L along a wide track to reach a road.

3. Turn L along the road; in $\frac{1}{4}$ mile cross with care to a side road on your R. In a few yards, cross a stile on your R by a footpath signpost and go along the LH field edge. Cross a stile by a metal gate; as the path descends, cross over a stile in an iron fence and shortly go over further stile in wooden fence. Go along the RH field edge and through an enclosed thicket via a stile, a long plank footbridge and squeeze posts. Continue along the RH field edge shortly crossing a stile and leave the field by a stile in the corner. Turn R along the enclosed track and in 300 yards on your R, cross a footbridge and stile. Cross the field diagonally to reach the road via a stile.

4. Cross with great care the dualled A30 to a footpath signpost opposite (to the R of the gas compound). Cross the stile and go along an enclosed path. Shortly cross a stile and keep along the RH edge of a large field passing a stile to enter an enclosed path via another stile to join a road at Hunters Hill.

5. Turn L along the road shortly passing Ferney Close (the home of Field Marshal Viscount Alanbrooke). On reaching West Green House, turn R at a footpath signpost opposite and take the ride through West Green Common to reach a road at The Dutch House. Turn R along the lane (mind traffic). Shortly at a sharp RH bend in the road, cross a stile on your L (by a footpath signpost) and go along the RH field edge. At a metal gate in front of you, turn R through a kissing gate, cross the drive diagonally L and go through the LH of two kissing gates. Turn L along the LH field edge, through a gap in the hedge, over a footbridge and stile; continue along the LH field edge. At the corner of the field, turn R and soon L over a stile, then keep to the LH field edge. Leave the field by a kissing gate and pass Hazeley Lodge to join a road.

6. Turn L along the road and shortly at a footpath signpost on your R, turn R along a footpath through a wood to reach another road. Turn R along the road and at the roundabout, turn L to return to the Waggon & Horses.

SHAPLEY **R**ANCH

MRS HUNTER

**01252
843414**

HORSE FODDER & EQUINE ACCESSORIES

VITAMINS, MINERALS, VETERINARY ITEMS, TACK AND RUGS

OPEN 7 DAYS A WEEK 9am TO 6pm
LONDON ROAD, PHOENIX GREEN,
HOOK, HANTS, RG27 8HY

Walk No 3   St MARY'S CHURCH, WINCHFIELD & SHAPLEY HEATH

[5 miles, 2½ hours]

1. Start from the Waggon & Horses, Hartley Wintney. Take the road with Hatten's Pond on your R and follow the tarmac path through the Trafalgar Oaks. Cross the road and go along Green Lane opposite passing more Trafalgar Oaks and the WI Hut on your L. At Oldfield View, keep ahead on a track through the oak trees. At Church View, turn L at footpath signpost and follow the track on the RH edge, go through squeeze posts to enter a large field. Leave the field by squeeze posts and cross the road to St Mary's Church opposite.

2. At the footpath signpost, turn R along a path through trees. At the two-fingered footpath signpost opposite Church House Farm, turn L over the stile and across the field. Cross a track and a bridge to squeeze posts opposite; go along the LH field edge, through further squeeze posts and down steps to a road. Turn R along the RHS of the road, just beyond South Cottage turn L over a stile by a footpath signpost and across a small field to turn L along the farm track and over the M3 bridge. Go through a gap by the LH metal gate, along an enclosed track and then follow the RH field edge to reach a road by a stile in the corner next to a telegraph pole.

3. Turn R along the RHS of the road, passing the Winchfield Inn. At the T-junction, turn L along Odiham Road and just before the railway bridge, cross the road with care to a footpath signpost opposite. Follow the enclosed path by the railway; descend steps, pass under the M3 and ascend steps to reach the old road to Potbridge.

4. Turn L along the old road and in 70 yards, turn R at a byway signpost into Shapley Heath. Go along the track and soon bear L at the farm gate on your R. At the next farm gate ahead of you, turn R down the descending track. In due course at the end of a large field on your R, turn R over a stile into the large field. Go along the LH field edge, cross a stile and soon go through an enclosed thicket via squeeze posts, a long plank bridge and a stile. Continue along the LH field edge; at a metal gate, cross a stile in a wooden fence and in a few yards, cross another stile in a metal fence and continue along the RH edge of a field. Cross a stile and leave the field by a stile next to a gate.

5. Cross with care the road ahead and turn L along the footway. At a footpath signpost on your R (opposite a sign to Ashley House), turn R at a footpath signpost and go along a track through a wood. Go through black and white posts, across a road and go along the footway on the RHS of Mitchell Avenue.   Shortly cross over Church View and keep ahead on the track through some oak trees. At Oakfield View go along Green Lane to return to the Waggon & Horses.

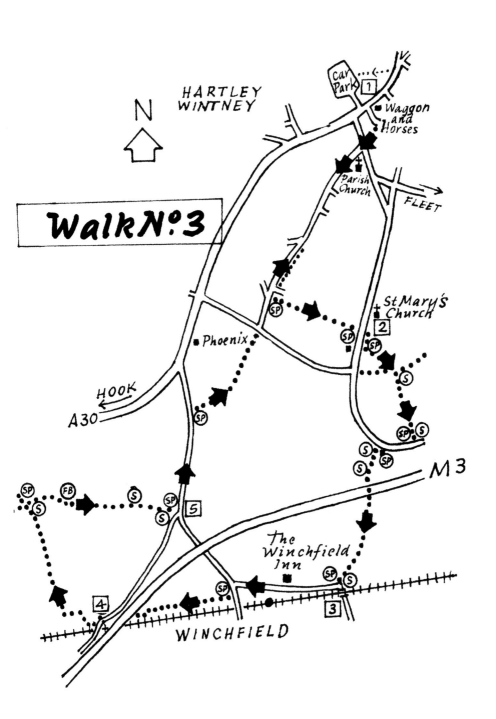

N

HARTLEY WINTNEY

Walk Nº 3

HOOK
A30

FLEET

Waggon and Horses

Parish Church

St Mary's Church

Phoenix

M 3

The Winchfield Inn

WINCHFIELD

Walk No 4   HAZELEY HEATH & DIPLEY

[5 miles, 2½ hours]

1. Start from the Lamb Hotel; go out of Hartley Wintney and fork L along Hunts Common road. Shortly just after Hunters Lodge, at a footpath signpost, turn L on an enclosed path between houses; go through a wooden gate to enter a wood. Keep ahead and bear right at a fork to reach a clearing on Hazeley Heath. Keep ahead on a wide gravel track, cross a concrete road and fork half R on a path across the heath. In ¼ mile reach some concrete bollards and turn R along a gravel leading to Purdies Farm.

2. Turn L on a track, then a path [can be muddy] on the edge of the wood with fields on your R. Pass Wedgewood Farm and at Crabtree Lodge, go ahead over a stile in a hedge, across a grass area and a pond outlet, finally over another stile. The path continues and in due course arrives at the lodge house of Bramshill Police College. Turn L up the road to the T-junction with the B3011.

3. Turn R and cross the road with care to descend on the lane to the Shoulder of Mutton. Before reaching the pub, turn L along the road to Mattingley and turn L again on the lane to Hazeley Bottom. At a L bend in the lane [blockhouse on your L], turn R at a footpath signpost through a kissing gate and cross the field to a stile opposite. Cross a footbridge and another stile and go along the LHS of a field, leave the field by a kissing gate in its corner.

4. Turn L along this road and in 100 yards, turn L at a footpath signpost * and over a stile by a gate. Go along the LHS of a field, over another stile and follow the LHS of the next field to a track. Keep ahead to a stile by a gate.

5. Cross the road to the track opposite. Go through a gap by a gate and along the LHS of a field to Sherwoods Farm. Turn R along the tarmac drive and at the end of the pond by a footpath signpost, turn hard L along RH edge of the grassed area (with hedge on your R). In 200 yards turn R over a concrete bridge with a handrail to enter a large field. Go along the LHS of this field and in its far corner go through a kissing gate, cross the drive to the RH of two kissing gates opposite. Go along the LHS side of the field and along an enclosed path next to a small gas pumping station to join West Green Road.

6. Turn L along the road and at Meadow Lane fork L at a footpath signpost on a path through some trees to reach the A30. Turn L along this road to return to Hartley Wintney.

*At the time of writing the next two stiles were by-passed by an unofficial permissive path.

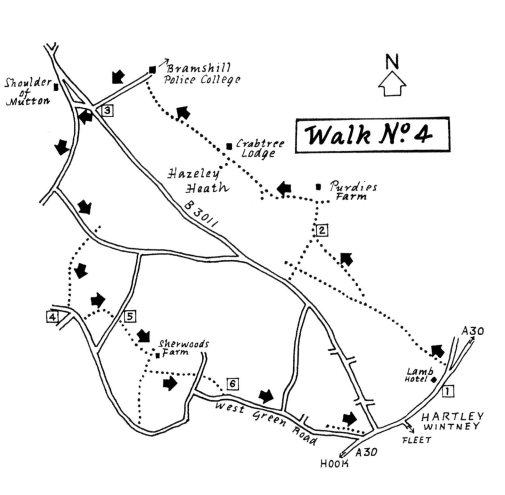

Walk Nº 4

Walk No 5   MATTINGLEY CHURCH & WEST GREEN HOUSE

[3 miles, 1¾ hours]

1. Start from Mattingley Church. Enter the churchyard by a footpath signpost, turn L and leave by a kissing gate in the corner of the churchyard. Turn R along an enclosed farm track (can be muddy); at a signpost, turn L through metal gates along an enclosed grass track. At the end of the track, cross a concrete bridge and go through the gate; turn half R across the field towards a large pylon. Keep ahead to a kissing gate and footbridge to follow the River Whitewater. Turn L, over a concrete bridge with a white handrail (close to Dipley Mill), and then over a sleeper bridge. Go ahead on a defined path and turn R at waymark post along the field edge to leave the field by a kissing gate.

2. Cross the road and go along the lane to Dipley Common. Bear L at a footpath signpost (opposite Dipley Farm) and go along the track to pass Dipley Springs. At Timbers, turn L and just beyond Woodside Cottage, take the enclosed path (footpath signpost). At the end of the enclosed path, turn R and soon pass a wood on your R; at the end of the field continue through a strip of woodland to a road.

3. Turn L along the road and R at the T-junction. At the LH bend in the road (just before West Green House) turn R through bushes and enter a field by a stile and footpath signpost. Go over a further stile and follow the path along the LH edge of the field. By the metal gate, go ahead by a line of oak trees, and leave the field by a metal gate.

4. Cross the road and take the track opposite to Dameles bungalow and then through a gap by a gate. At the green hut, turn L and shortly R down the grass track. At the bottom of the descending track, turn L along the path. In 100 yards, turn R over a footbridge and stile by a metal gate to go along the LH field edge to reach and cross the River Whitewater by a footbridge.

5. Go ahead across the field and turn R along the LH field edge (away from the river). Just beyond a metal water trough, turn L over a stile by a wooden gate and go along an enclosed path. Cross the next stile (by a wooden gate), turn L and then R through metal gates along track to reach the road via a stile by a gate. Turn R along the road on the RH verge (watch traffic) to pass the Leather Bottle. Turn R at Dipley Road (sign to West Green House) and in a few yards L at footpath signpost to go along the drive passing Fosters. Keep ahead on the path through trees, cross a drive and continue with a wall on your R. Mattingley Church appears at the end of the track.

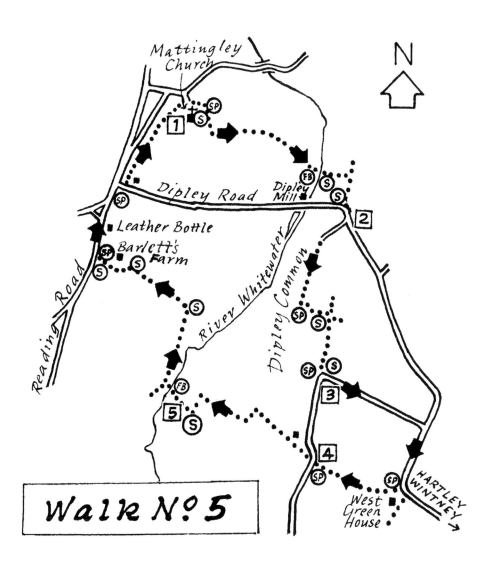

Mattingley Church

N

Dipley Road

Dipley Mill

Leather Bottle

Barlett's Farm

River Whitewater

Reading Road

Dipley Common

West Green House

HARTLEY WINTNEY

Walk Nº 5

Walk No 6   ROTHERWICK, TYLNEY HALL & NEWNHAM GREEN

[4 ½ miles, 2 ¼ hours]

1. Start from the White Hart, Hook. Go along Reading Road on the footway and turn L into Goose Lane then follow the enclosed track and tarmac path to reach and cross road.

2. Bear slightly L to go over a footbridge and a kissing gate to follow the LHS of a large field. At the corner of the field, go through a kissing gate and turn R along an enclosed path. Continue ahead through a wood, through another kissing gate and along the RHS of a large field. Keep ahead on the descending path heading to the RHS of a white house. Cross a footbridge and shortly go through a kissing gate to reach and cross Runten's Lane. At the waymark post opposite, go along the LHS of the field and at the corner of the wood, bear R across the field on a defined track to reach a road.
[Turn R for Rotherwick Village Hall and The Falcon]

3. Turn L along the road passing the Coach & Horses on your L and the village school and church on your R. Just beyond a post box, bear L on the path between the pond and houses. Turn L along the road and shortly at a footpath signpost, go up the drive to Tylney Park Golf Club. Before the clubhouse, turn R at a footpath signpost along a road to the Optrex Business Park.

4. At the entrance to the business park, turn L at a PUBLIC FOOTPATH notice and go across the golf course. Cross the fairways with care (watching out for golfers), aiming to the L of two large trees and then towards the corner of a wood by a white signboard and a footpath signpost. Keep ahead on the LH edge of the golf course. Enter a wood on a path [Look out for surprise view of Tylney Hall on your L] which in due course bears R leading to a green gate. Follow ahead on the road that leads to Park Lane and the Old House at Home pub at Newnham Green. [Newnham Church lies to the R of Newnham Green]

5. Cross the Green on its LH side, go over the road and at a footpath signpost by a large willow tree to the R of Tithe Barn, enter the enclosed Church Path to Hook. Pass a wooden barrier, and go along the LH field edge, across the field on a defined path, over a plank bridge and up steps to a gate and cross a concrete road. Keep to the left of the hedge for 15 yards, then turn R over a stile and along the LH edge of the field to go through a kissing gate and the road to Owen's Farm.

6. Cross the stile opposite and follow the RH edge of the field; turn R over a footbridge and L over another footbridge. Go straight ahead following a fenced path. Cross a tarmac path and along an enclosed path to turn L along a lane. Cross Froud's Close, keep ahead on a tarmac path through trees and along Newnham Road to return to Hook.

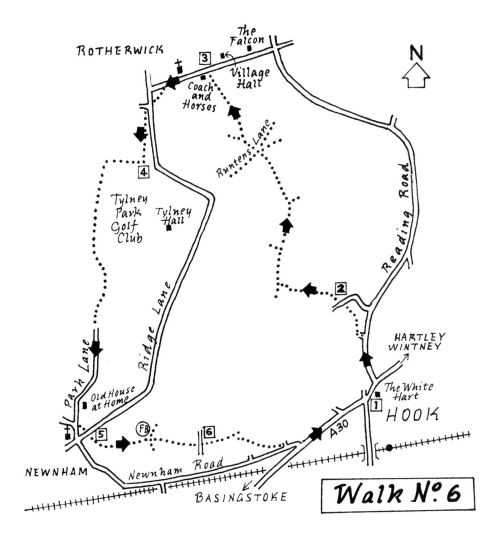

15

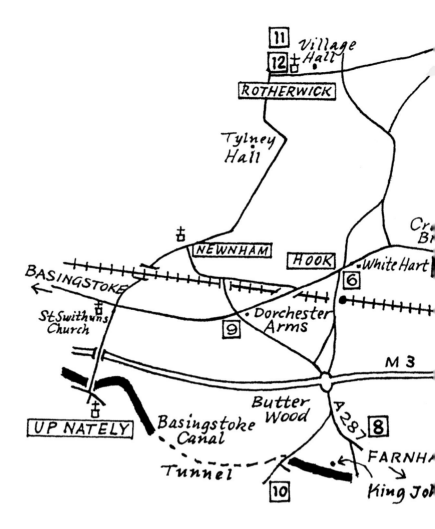

MAP SHOWING
WALKS STARTS 1 – 12
&
POINTS OF INTEREST

N

11 Village Hall
12 ✝
ROTHERWICK

Tylney Hall

✝
NEWNHAM   HOOK   •White Hart

BASINGSTOKE   **6**

St.Swithuns Church   • Dorchester Arms
9

M 3

Butter Wood   A287   **8**

✝
UP NATELY   Basingstoke Canal   FARNHA

Tunnel

10   King Jo

Cr Br

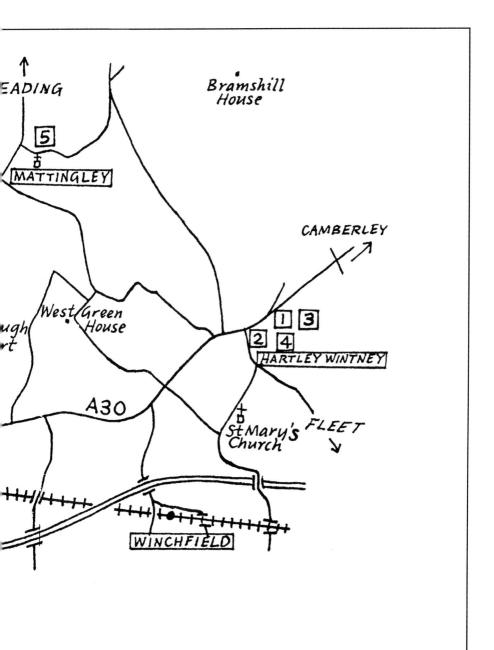

Walk No 7   RIVER WHITEWATER & BOROUGH COURT

[3½ miles, 1¾ hours]

1. Start from the Crooked Billet on the A30 east of Hook. Go along the road to the L of the pub to Whitewater Mill and fork L at the Mill by a footpath signpost on your L, go along an enclosed path. Cross a stile and go along the LHS of a large field. Cross a stile near to a farm gate (do NOT cross the bridge on your R) but bear R over a field and cross the River Whitewater by a footbridge on your R.

2. Cross a small field and go over a stile and footbridge opposite. Bear R through a small paddock and go through gates. At a footpath signpost by Borough Court, turn L up a track. Just before a large wooden shed on your L, turn R and then L along an enclosed track, go through a 5-bar gate to reach a road.
NOTE: To visit West Green House Garden continue on the footpath opposite

3. Turn R along the road. A little beyond Borough Court lodge on your R, turn L at footpath signpost, over a stile and along a track and a further stile to enter an old orchard. Leave the orchard by another stile and shortly cross a stile on your R and go along the LHS of the field. Leave the field by a stile in its corner and cross with great care the dualled A30 to a byway signpost opposite on your L.

4. Go along the enclosed grass track and after 250 yards, turn R over a footbridge and go half L across a field to a stile to enter a small field. Cross this field to a footbridge and stile opposite. Go along the LHS of a large field, through a kissing gate and follow the wire fence on your L to a stile. Cross the next field to a stile to the R of a large pylon.

5. Descend the bank and turn R along the road and at Totters Farm, turn L at a footpath signpost, over a stile and a small field to a further stile. Continue ahead over a field to cross a protected electrified wire. Keep ahead across a large field aiming to the RH end of a line of trees. Go through a gap in the hedge and follow the hedge on your R; at its corner, turn R and go along RHS of the field. Go over a stile by a gate and over a field to another stile in a wire fence. With the fence on your L and then the River Whitewater, go through a kissing gate in the field corner to cross the busy A30 to return to the Crooked Billet.

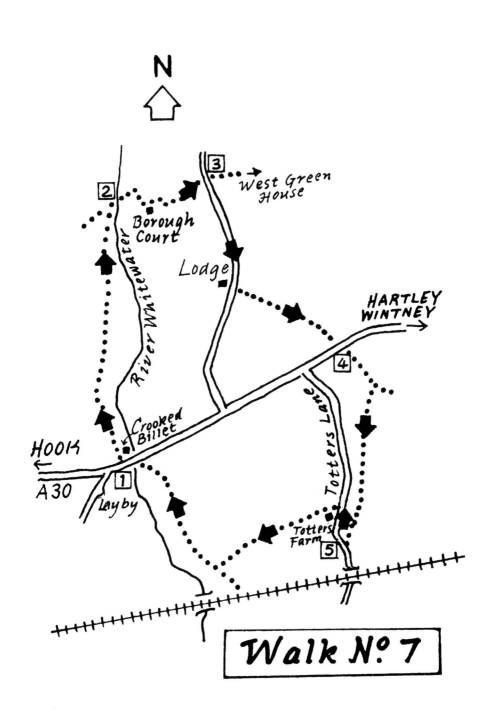

N

West Green House

Borough Court

River Whitewater

Lodge

HARTLEY WINTNEY

Crooked Billet

HOOK

A30

Layby

Totters Lane

Totters Farm

Walk Nº 7

Walk No 8 KING JOHN'S CASTLE, GREYWELL HILL PARK & BUTTERWOOD

[$3\frac{1}{2}$ miles, $1\frac{3}{4}$ hours]

1. Start from Bartley Heath Pottery. Go through a gap to the L of a metal barrier and along the old road (ignoring the bike track on the L). At the embankment, cross a stile and footbridge on the L, up steps, over a stile and cross with great care the dualled A287 to the footpath signpost opposite. Descend the steps, cross a stile, over a footbridge and go along the path ahead. At a 3-fingered signpost, turn L along track (keep to the RH drier path by the ponds) and emerge from the copse. Bear R to go through concrete bollards and a wooden gate, pass houses and a further gate by a cattle grid to join a lane.

2. Turn R along the lane, over a footbridge and through a wooden gate (by a cattle grid) to cross the River Whitewater. Just beyond Castle Mill House at a footpath signpost on your R, go through a kissing gate and cross a small field and through a further kissing gate to reach the canal towpath. Turn R along the towpath (passing King John's Castle), over the River Whitewater aqueduct, arriving at the entrance to the Greywell tunnel. Turn L over the tunnel portal to join the road.

3. Turn R along the road and shortly R again at the T-junction. Cross the road to a footpath signpost opposite. Follow the enclosed path and cross the stile to enter Greywell Hill Park. Turn R and follow the RH edge of the park, cross a stile to enter Butterwood. Keep ahead and go through squeeze posts and turn R along a bridleway. Just beyond a small pond on your R, go through squeeze posts (by a wooden gate on the L) and along a wide track. In due course, cross a long plank footbridge (to the L of a boggy area) and keep ahead passing a waymark post. Just beyond this, at another waymark post the path veers to the R to pass another waymark post and follow a wide track. Eventually, at another waymark post, bear L into the trees, and then bear R at the next junction and waymark post. Go through a gap (by a metal gate and a white house) to cross a lane to a footpath signpost opposite. Follow the footpath, over a small footbridge and stile to reach a road.

4. Cross the road and over the stile opposite. In a few yards at 3-fingered signpost turn L along the path and up and over the A287 to return to the Bartley Heath Pottery. NOTE: If this path was wet on your way out, use the road on your return.

ALTERNATIVE: The walk may be shortened by half an hour by parking in Greywell and joining at point 3 (see map). At point 4 cross the road and the 3-fingered signpost go straight ahead, then follow the description in point 1 towards point 2 (see map).

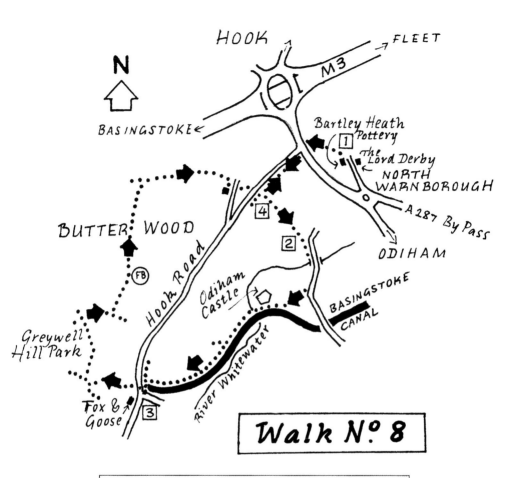

Walk Nº 8

BARTLEY HEATH
POTTERY

North Warnborough, Hook, Hampshire.

A large range of handmade and decorated pots
made by Lesley and Michael Dixon.
Commissions taken for
Commemorative Plates, House Plaques, and Named Mugs.

Telephone, 01256 702163

www.bartleyheathpottery.co.uk

Walk No 9   BUTTERWOOD, GREYWELL TUNNEL & LYDE RIVER

[4 ½ miles, 2 ½ hours]

1. Start from the Dorchester Arms on the A30 west of Hook. Go along Holly Bush Lane and pass Hollybush View; keep on the track through the trees to reach Heather Lane. Turn L along the lane and over the M3 bridge.

2. Turn L at the footpath signpost, go over a stile and follow the wooden fence by the M3. Look out for a waymark on the fence and then turn R to enter Butterwood. Go ahead on the wide track passing a large beech tree and waymark post. 100 yards ahead, fork R at a waymark post. Ignore a R turn at a large oak tree and keep ahead passing another waymark post. At a T-junction, turn R by a waymark post and go along a path leading to a clearing. Turn L at another waymark post and down a wide track; at the bottom of the slope, cross a track, over a footbridge and on a path through some trees to reach a bridleway. Turn R along a bridleway; in 350 yards turn R down a permissive path and descend to the Basingstoke Canal towpath by the western portal of the Greywell Tunnel.

3. Go along the towpath under Eastrop Bridge and Slade's Bridge. Then cross a footbridge over the Nately Brickworks Arm of the canal and turn L along the towpath. Go under the next bridge, turn L up some steps to the road.

4. Turn L along this road and over the M3 bridge. At a gap in the road barrier on your L by a bridleway signpost, turn hard L down a track. Turn R at a metal gate along a track shortly on the edge of a wood. In due course this bridleway reaches a road. Turn R along the road (with the River Lyde on your L) to reach, and cross the dualled A30 with great care (Red Lion on your L).
NOTE: St Swithun`s Church can be reached by turning R along the A30, turn R at a signpost, cross a field to the church.

5. At a byway signpost, go under a metal barrier and along an enclosed track leading to Crown Lane. Turn L along this lane, under the railway bridge to reach Newnham Green.

6. At the cross roads, go opposite along Ridge Lane; in 50 yards just before Tithe Barn, turn R at a large willow tree by a footpath signpost and along the enclosed Church Path. Pass under a barrier, go along the LHS of the field and then across the field and a long plank bridge, up some steps to a concrete road. Turn R through a metal gate (if locked use nearby stile in hedge) and go along the RHS of the field to a stile in its corner. Follow an enclosed path to a road. Cross the road to the Old School Road, over the railway bridge and along the road to cross with great care the dualled A30 to return to the Dorchester Arms.

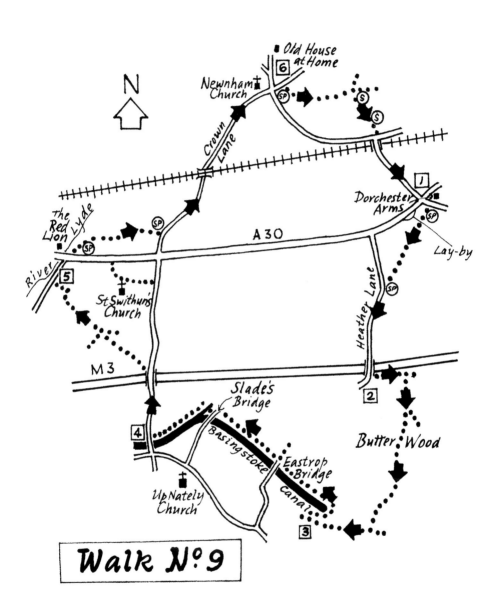

N

Old House at Home

Newnham Church

6

Crown Lane

The Red Lion

Lyde

River

5

St Swithun's Church

A 30

Dorchester Arms

J

Lay-by

Heather Lane

SP

M 3

Slade's Bridge

2

Butter Wood

4

Basingstoke Canal

Eastrop Bridge

Up Nately Church

3

Walk Nº 9

Walk No 10   GREYWELL & BUTTERWOOD

[3 miles, 1 ½ hours]

1. Start from Greywell Village Hall. Go along the road towards the Fox & Goose for a few yards, at a footpath signpost on your L, go through squeeze posts and along RHS of a field. Turn R, then L along field edge (ignore squeeze posts into sunken thicket); keep along the field edge and go through squeeze posts in the field corner. Turn L over a stile and then go along the RHS of Greywell Hill Park.

2. Enter Butterwood by a stile, follow a path that shortly crosses a bridleway through 2 squeeze posts. Keep ahead on the path, ignoring side turnings; go over a crossing track by waymark post. Pass a further waymark post and at next waymark post, fork L and in 100 yards, join a wide track. Go ahead on wide track, and soon turn R along a track passing two sheds. Follow this track ignoring all side turnings eventually to leave Butterwood by a metal barrier at the old road [white house on your R]. Cross the road to a footpath signpost opposite on your R and soon reach the Hook Road via a stile.

3. Cross the road and over the stile opposite to enter Bartley Heath & North Warnborough Greens.   At the 3-fingered signpost, turn R over a stile and follow along RHS of the fields [with Hook Road on your R]. In due course pass behind a white house and, at a row of houses, go through squeeze posts to join Hook Road for a short distance.

4. At a footpath signpost on your L by Dorchester Way, go through squeeze posts, across a small field and stile to follow the RHS of the next fields [houses on your R]. Go through 2 sets of squeeze posts, then bear L by barns, through squeeze posts and over the Basingstoke Canal tunnel portal to reach a road. Turn R then L along The Street, passing the Fox & Goose to return to Greywell Village Hall.

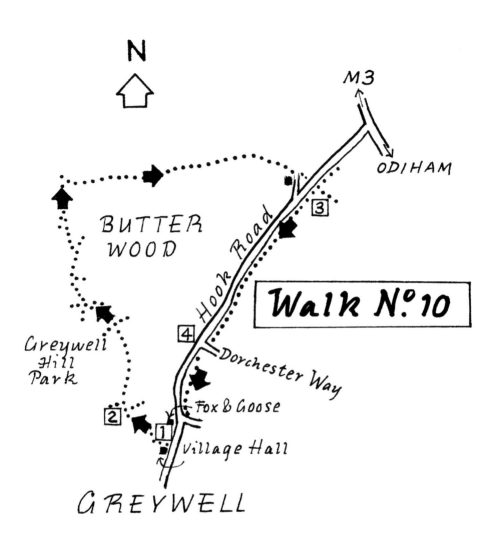

N

M3

ODIHAM

BUTTER
WOOD

Hook Road

③

Walk Nº 10

④

Greywell
Hill
Park

Dorchester Way

②

① Fox & Goose

Village Hall

GREYWELL

THE FOX & GOOSE
GREYWELL
Your "real" village local
OPEN all day 7 days a week serving fine ales
& good food
Real Devonshire Clotted Cream Teas
Large car park & children's play areas
The FOX & GOOSE 01256 702062
All a good country pub should be

Walk No 11   BLACK WOOD & LYDE GREEN

[3 ¾ miles, 2 hours]

1. Start from Rotherwick Church; leave the rear of the churchyard by a kissing gate, turn R along the field and shortly bear half L across the field. At the field corner, cross a track and go through two kissing gates and across a field to another kissing gate opposite. Turn R along an enclosed path and keep along the LHS of a large field. Leave the field by a kissing gate in its corner and across a small field to another kissing gate. Go along the drive and shortly turn L along the lane. Do not go along Lampards Close, but keep ahead on an enclosed path. Go through a kissing gate and turn R along a shingle drive to reach a road.

2. Turn L along Wedmans Lane and shortly turn R along a track passing some houses. Enter Black Wood by a kissing gate; ignore all side turnings and leave the wood by kissing gate, cross a footbridge and through squeeze posts. Go along the RHS of a small field to a stile in a white gate. Do not cross the stile to Bottle Lane.

3. Turn L along an enclosed path; at a waymark post by a metal gate, keep ahead along the RHS of a long field. Cross a bridleway (by a waymark post) to a stile opposite. Go along the RHS of a large field. As the field narrows, head for a wooden barrier and stile at the far end. Go over stile and through a gate to cross a footbridge to reach Lyde Green and a road.

4. Turn R along the road and shortly look out for a footpath signpost on your L and cross the field to continue along the RHS of the field [beside Rotherwick Lane]. Continue along the RHS of another field. Cross a stile, keep ahead as the path soon descends. At the corner of the next field, by squeeze posts at a footpath signpost, turn L along the RHS of the field. Go through a gap a few yards to the L of the field corner and along the RHS of the next field. At the field corner, turn L and then R along the RHS of another field; cross a stile and footbridge to reach a road.

5. Turn L along Mill Lane. Pass Winnells on your L and shortly go through a gap on your R and turn L along the LHS of a large field. At the corner of the wood, turn L at a stile and go up a track. Keep ahead on the track between fields to reach and cross a road to a stile opposite. Bear half R across the field to enter the churchyard by a kissing gate.

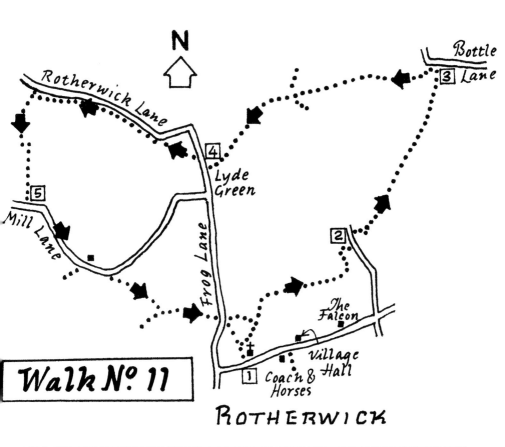

Walk Nº 11

ROTHERWICK

Coach & Horses

Chris & Kelly

Opening Hours: Monday Closed
Tue - Fri, 12-2pm
Sat - Sun, Open All Day

Choice of Real Ales, Fine Wines, Beer Garden, Log Fires, Children & Dogs Welcome.
Bookings Highly Recommended

The Street, Rotherwick, Hampshire, RG27 9BG
Telephone: 01256 762542   Email: ch-rotherwick@hotmail.com

Walk No 12   HALL'S LANE & LYDE GREEN

[3 $\frac{1}{2}$ miles, 1$\frac{3}{4}$ hours]

1. Start from Rotherwick Church and go along The Street passing the Coach & Horses, the Village Hall and The Falcon. At the cross roads, turn L along Wedmans Lane and keep ahead on the bridleway. In $\frac{1}{2}$ mile, cross a footpath (waymark post), and continue along Hall's Lane (can be muddy) to reach a road.

2. Turn L along the road and at a sharp RH bend in the road turn L at a footpath signpost along a track. In 150 yards at a gap on your L, leave the track and immediately turn R along the path through a tree belt (see waymark). After $\frac{1}{4}$ mile at a T-junction by a waymark post, turn L along a path and in 100 yards look out for and go through a gap on your L. Follow along the RH field edge, turning L and R at corners of the wood. Cross a stile and follow along the RH field edge. At the field corner, cross a stile by a gate and go along the LH field edge. Go over the stile in the field corner and across another field. Cross a stile to the L of a black barn, over the lawn by Poplars Farm to reach the road.

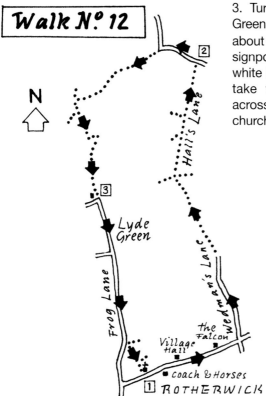

3. Turn L along the road through Lyde Green. Keep ahead on Frog Lane for about $\frac{1}{2}$ mile and look out for a footpath signpost on your L just beyond a large white house on your L. Turn L (do not take the track) and go diagonally across a field to enter Rotherwick churchyard by a kissing gate.

POINTS OF INTEREST

Hartley Wintney

Cricketers Green and the Trafalgar Oaks The Green lies in the centre of the village to the south of the High Street alongside the Cricketers Inn. Cricket has been played there since 1770. Hatten's Pond was named after Robert Hatton, landlord of the nearby Waggon & Horses until 1903. The Trafalgar Oaks were planted on common land in 1807 by Lady Mildmay in response to Admiral Collingswood's appeal to provide timber for future Royal Navy ships. The ironclads saved the oaks, although more recent storms blew some done. These have been replaced retaining the original geometric pattern of the oaks.

[Walk Nos. 2 & 3]

WI Hut off Green Lane is an ex-Army hut acquired by Mrs Bigwither in 1919 following the end of the 1914-18 War. She was taken down to Salisbury Plain by one of her employees. The hut was put on ground belonging to the Calthorpe family in whose hands it remained until 1948 when it was then purchased by Elizabeth Huntingdon Moore and given to the Women's Institute (WI) in memory of her friend Adeline Bernal. During the thirties it was used by the Mothers Union and for wedding receptions, etc. During the 1939 - 45 War it was used as a mess hall by the Canadian Elgin Regiment - the cookhouse foundations were uncovered when the ground was prepared for the car park some years ago. The Canadians slept in tents dotted around the common under the Trafalgar Oaks. The Canadians left in 1944. After the war it returned to its traditional use which then included school dinners. The WI Hut is now widely used by many organisations including a thriving Country Market on Friday mornings.

[Walk No. 3]

St Mary's Church has a 700 year old nave and chancel; the flint tower and brick transepts were added in the 19th century. The church contains a 1636 communion table, an ancient iron-bound chest and medieval wall paintings portraying contemporary village dress. Robert Ray a prosperous shopkeeper who died in 1677, left in his will arrangements for sixty ells of cloth to be distributed every Good Friday to widows and widowers of the parish. He stipulated the cloth should be bought at ye shoppe where I now Live in Hartley Wintney. The board recording his charity is on the west wall of the nave. On the other side of the west door are the Royal Arms of Queen Anne, the last Stuart monarch, dated 1705 showing the Stuart shield she used from 1702 to 1706 before the Act of Union with Scotland necessitated a further change in the Royal Arms. From 1234 to 1870 St Mary's was the parish church, but it proved too small for the growing population and was replaced in 1870 by St John the Evangelist Church on the village green. The Church is no longer used for regular worship and is maintained by the Redundant Church fund. It can be visited by obtaining the key. St Mary's Churchyard is beautifully situated and contains the tomb of Field Marshal Viscount Alanbrooke, Chief of the Imperial General Staff 1941-46. It is inscribed, "Remembering with gratitude his life of service, his leadership in War and his love of nature".

[Walk Nos. 2 & 3]

West Green House, the Old Manor of West Green, is an early 18th century redbrick house that was lived in by the notorious General (Hangman) Henry Hawley who rivalled Judge Jeffreys for his cruelty. He commanded the victorious army at Culloden in 1746 and subsequently he set up gibbets in Scotland for the vanquished. He returned to West Green House and died in 1759. His Will said: My carcass may be put anywhere, tis equal to me. He and his descendents were buried in the vault below the chancel of St Mary's, Hartley Wintney. West Green House was presented to the National Trust in 1957 by Sir Victor Sasson. The four 18th century walled gardens, with flower borders and potagers, are encircled by water gardens studded with neo-classical follies, cages and monuments. The gardens have recently been carefully restored and can be visited in season.

[Walk Nos 2, 5 &7]

Bramshill

Bramshill House was built by Lord Zouche between 1605 and 1612. It has hardly been altered since and is one of the finest examples of Jacobean architecture in England. It commands wide views from over 300ft as befits its name which means, broom covered hill. The Cope family lived there until 1936; in their time mummers performed their ancient play every Christmas. Lord Brocket, the last private owner, sold it in 1953; it is now the Police College and is not open to the public. In 1621 George Abbet, the Archbishop of Canterbury, came to Lord Zouche's fine new house to consecrate the chapel. He was entertained to a deer-hunt and unfortunately killed the keeper, Peter Hawkins, with his cross-bow instead of the deer which was being presented to him as an easy target. It is said that Peter Hawkins had been warned the Archbishop was a bad shot and the Coroner's Inquest curious verdict was: misadventure and his own fault. The Archbishop did penance of various forms for the rest of his life. The fatal accident took place under an oak tree known from then on as the Keeper's Oak and this magnificent old pollard tree survived until a few years ago. Recently the present Archbishop of Canterbury deputised the Bishop of Winchester to plant an oak sapling taken from the Keeper's Oak so maintaining the historical link.

[Walk No 4]

Hook and Newnham

Borough Court The core of the building is a large medieval 5-bay timber-framed manor hall with a Tudor block on its northern side. It has a fine set of Elizabethan brick chimneys. Anne Boleyn, who had changed her name from Bullen, had some connection with Borough Court. In 1906 the manor hall was extended and divided into several floors; a service wing was added. It is a private residence.

[Walk No7]

St Nicholas Church, Newnham was rebuilt in 1846-7 and retains much of the original Norman church including the chancel arch, north and south walls and the doorway. A Saxon-style tower replaced the original bell turret. The three bells date from about 1500, 1602 and 1662. In the 18th century, the bells were rung on Guy Fawkes Day and the Coronation anniversary to re-affirm loyalty. Earliest references to the church date from about 1125-35, and it contains a list of rectors from 1303. The church has no memorials earlier then the 1800s, they were probably lost during the 19th century rebuilding. The Church Path from Hook crosses Newnham Green and was built to provide a dry passage.

[Walk Nos 6 & 9]

St Swithun's Church, Nately Scures was built late in the 12th century. It is probably the most perfect example of a single cell Norman church in the country, with a sole entrance on the north side. It is built of flint rubble with angle quorns, the door and window dressings are of Binstead stone. The Mermaid legend of Nately Scures tells how a sailor forsook a mermaid for a Nately Scures girl. On his wedding day, the mermaid carried him away down Water End to the sea. Sir Guy Carleton, the first Lord Dorchester who served under Wolfe in Canada, is buried in the Carleton vault as is his brother, General Thomas Carleton, Governor of New Brunswick.

[Walk No 9]

The White Hart, Hook. The original building, now hidden by a Georgian facade, is thought to be of medieval origin. It has been known by several names since the 17th century: The Bell, The Spreadeagle, The Wyvern and since 1840, The White Hart. It was a staging post at the crossroads of the London to Exeter and the Reading to Gosport turnpikes. The connection with the sea suggests some of the timbers may have been originally used in ships. The White Hart has its own restored brew house and maltings in an adjoining building. Nearby was a road-wagon station which repaired stagecoaches.

[Walk No 6]

Mattingley

The Church, has no patron saint possibly as the 14th century building was originally a moot hall or maybe a chapel of ease. In 1425 Pope Martin granted a licence for a cemetery as people found it inconvenient to carry their dead to Heckfield as the land between was often flooded. Bishop Wayneflete is believed to have founded the present church which was probably started towards the end of the 15th century. Parallelogram-shaped bricks, possibly from Hazeley Heath, were used in a timber frame for the herringbone effect. In 1837 the nave was widened and the present porch added. The ancient font was recently moved back to the church from the churchyard which has an enormous Celtic Cross.

[Walk No 5]

Rotherwick

The Church, has no patron saint. Rotherwick derives from the Saxon words meaning cattle enclosure. The oldest part of the church is the late 13th century flint and stone chancel, but the font bowl may date from the early 12th century. The original musicians` gallery is at the west end of the 15th century nave; it has an access door from the clock chamber. The 17th century tower has six bells, one being 14th century and the second oldest in the country. The church contains the Tylney monuments. The tower wall is pitted probably by musket practice during the Napoleonic Wars.

[Walk Nos 6, 11 & 12]

Tylney Hall was first built in 1700 by Frederick Tylney; the layout of the approaches has been likened to the Palace of Versailles. The grass avenue to the west is seen from the golf course. The hall gradually deteriorated and in 1878 Charles Harris began rebuilding the hall. This was altered by Sir Lionel Phillips around 1900 to the present hall which resembles the former hall and contains some of the former decoration. Tylney Hall was used as a hospital during the 1914-18 War. It was bought in 1919 by Major Cayzer, the shipping magnate, who became Lord Rotherwick. During the Second World War it was the Headquarters of his Clan Shipping Line. In 1946 it became a special school finally run by Brent Council. It is now an hotel.

[Walk No 6]

The Village Hall was built in 1931 as a memorial to a young American, Charles de Forest, son of Mr & Mrs Henry de Forest. They rented Tylney Hall for two months each year from Sir Herbert Cayzer and they were well liked and respected locally. In 1929 Charles de Forest left Rotherwick to go on a world cruise. His parents shortly received the shattering news that he had died of a fever in Italy. In 1930 Mr de Forest decided, because of his connection with Rotherwick, he would like to give something useful to the local people as a memorial to his son and he suggested a Village Hall. After a public meeting in 1931, construction started in January 1932 and was completed by October 1932 at a cost of £ 8000.

[Walk Nos. 6 & 12]

The Basingstoke Canal and Greywell Tunnel

Greywell tunnel is 1230 yards long and was completed in 1794 as a vital section of the **Basingstoke Canal**. The tunnel was dug under Greywell Hill Park because of objections to the original route proposed via Tylney Hall, Rotherwick. Bargees had to leg their way through the tunnel whilst horses were led over the hill on a bridleway whose route can still be followed. The eastern end of the tunnel has been restored and its portal can be seen from the towpath. The western portal of the tunnel has not been restored, but it is visible from a nearby permissive footpath that runs from the bridleway and above the restored embankment to the towpath. The canal originally went from the western end of the Greywell Tunnel to the canal basin at Basingstoke - now the site of the bus station. The section of the canal from this tunnel portal to site of the former Penney Bridge on the Greywell Road still contains some water, but it is not navigable. This section of the canal was bought by Hampshire County Council in 1990 and has been restored with the help of the Canal Society. In 1897 a 100 yard long Brickworks Arm was built for Up Nately Brickworks and the canal used to transport bricks for the Aldershot Camp barracks. The brickworks ceased in 1908 due to local clay producing inferior bricks.

[Walk Nos 8, 9 & 10]

River Whitewater

The river flows northwards from its source at Bidden Water, Greywell under the Basingstoke Canal by an aqueduct close to King John's Castle at North Warnborough, via Poland Mill, Odiham and through Hook passing the Crooked Billet pub and Borough Court to Dipley Mill, both are private residences. It continues under the Mattingley Clapper's Bridge to join the River Blackwater on the Hampshire/Berkshire border to form the Broadwater that finally joins the River Loddon at Swallowfield.

[Walk Nos 5, 7 & 8]

North Warnborough

King John's Castle lies beside the Basingstoke Canal. The Castle was built between 1207 and 1212 and was used by King John as a hunting lodge. It is reputed that King John set out from the castle in 1215 to sign the Magna Carta at Runnymede. The Dauphin laid siege to the Castle in 1216 and the garrison of 14 men held out for 14 days without losing a man and they were allowed to retain their freedom. David Bruce, King of Scotland, was held prisoner in the castle for 11 years from 1346. Only the keep of the castle now remains.

[Walk No 8]

Bartley Heath and North Warnborough Greens are a large area of heath, grassland and woodland. They were grazed for many centuries by local commoners' stock and were a vital part of the local economy. The North Warnborough Greens are lush, wet meadows by the clear chalk stream or the River Whitewater.

[Walk Nos 8 & 10]